CW00847996

THE UNBELIEVING HUSBAND

Out of Darkness and Into the Light

AN EXPERIENCE OF GRACE

1 Corinthians 7:14

In Loving Memory of My Husband Bill Gray

MARGE GRAY

WestBow Press books may be ordered through booksellers or by contacting:

WestBow Press
A Division of Thomas Nelson & Zondervan
1663 Liberty Drive
Bloomington, IN 47403
www.westbowpress.com
1 (866) 928-1240

ISBN: 978-1-9736-7083-4 (sc)
ISBN: 978-1-9736-7084-1 (hc)
ISBN: 978-1-9736-7082-7 (e)

Library of Congress Control Number: 2019910714

Print information available on the last page.

WestBow Press rev. date: 9/9/2019

DEDICATION

This book is dedicated to our one, true God and Father, to His Son Jesus Christ and to the Holy Spirit. Thank You that You hear -- and answer -- our prayers, particularly my prayer and the prayers of many for my husband's salvation. You are so wonderful!

To my husband Bill and the joy you gave me to watch you pray to Jesus. Just thinking about it makes me smile and love you all the more, knowing that you are in His army now.

1 CORINTHIANS 7:14

For the unbelieving husband is sanctified by the wife, and the unbelieving wife is sanctified by the husband: else were your children unclean; but now are they holy.

CONTENTS

Acknowledgements .... *xi*

Foreword ....*xv*

Introduction ....*xix*

CHAPTER 1 *THE EXPERIENCE* *1*

CHAPTER 2 *THE MESSAGE* *33*

CHAPTER 3 *WHO ARE WE?* *37*

CHAPTER 4 *WHAT DOES GOD WANT US TO KNOW?* *43*

To Those Who Believe **43**

To Those Who Do Not Believe **45**

To Everyone.. **46**

CHAPTER 5 WHAT DOES IT MEAN TO "BE SAVED?"......................................*47*

Saved FROM What?.................................... 48

Saved FOR What?...................................... 49

What Do I Need To Do To Be Saved?.......... 50

SCRIPTURE REFERENCES......................................*53*

FOR FURTHER INFORMATION *63*

YOUR GRACE EXPERIENCE JOURNEY NOTES.......... *65*

ACKNOWLEDGEMENTS

Thanks God, for getting me up at 1 AM on Monday, June 24, 2013 to type "The Experience" chapter for You. You know I could not have written this, but I'm thankful You did, for Your glory Lord. Thank You, Jesus!

Thank you, Andrea, my wonderful Christian granddaughter, for your listening to the Lord for the book cover. Thank you for being my spiritual inspiration as well as my spiritual warrior, for me and for Pawpaw.

Brother Ed, my constant friend for Bill's salvation, thank you for your prayers and the Foreword for the book. I am so glad you saw the before and after, the old man and the new man.

I also thank all of my family, friends, bowling buddies and strangers who prayed for Bill, my unbelieving husband for over thirty-two years.

Kerry, I'm thankful God has blessed you to help me get this book out so quickly. Many souls can be blessed with God's personal message to them sooner.

Follow up - March 2014

Thanks to all of you who have read the initial version of this book and for sharing God's message in it with others. I know some of you have read it multiple times. Thank you for your testimony of God's blessings you received from it.

At the end of Chapter 1 The Experience, "Several times before he died, I would pat his hand and tell him that his experience would give many others hope, many would be saved, and that we would get his experience out to people all over the world."

I had no idea that God would be publishing a book about it - this book.

Since the book was published in October 2013, it has been downloaded or purchased in the United Kingdom, Canada, India, Spain, Germany and the United States.

Even before Bill died, God had already planned to get His message out to others:

- His message of hope,
- His message of His faithfulness when we ask Him with all our heart, and
- His message of our individual choice determining where we will spend eternity

Follow up – August 2018

During an extended mission trip to Sri Lanka in April of 2017, the Lord had me share this book with a few of the local people there. I received feedback that they wanted to get the book translated into one their local languages – Sinhalese.

Praise the Lord! The book has been translated and published in Sri Lanka!

FOREWORD

At the time of this writing, my wife, Rebecca, and I have known Marge Gray for approximately seven plus years. This is around the time we joined the staff of Smyrna River of Life Assembly of God.

Marge has always possessed a most kind and gentle, loyal, generous and loving spirit. She is a true friend with a beautiful Christ-like life and demeanor. I think because of her consistent optimism and her consistent cheerfulness, we, and others of her closest friends and acquaintances never really knew the burdens she was bearing – the ridicule, criticism, opposition and spiritual assault at home on her walk with the Lord, and desire to have a Christian marriage.

She, along with countless other wives, has been a true and shining example of the believing wife with an unbelieving husband described in 1 Corinthians 7:14. Every time she even wanted to attend church where they lived, he was diametrically opposed to her going. However, when they moved to Smyrna, TN, just before we met her, she visited River of Life Church. She told Bill she wanted to attend and worship at River of Life. He finally agreed to *let* her attend.

Everyone found Bill likeable, personable, and enjoyed being around him - except when his voice and language was loud and abusive which proved to be embarrassing, usually at the times he was drinking. When drinking he would undergo a real personality change. And in those times he was very difficult to be around.

When they were at home, if anyone came to visit from the church, he would leave the room. Anytime the subject of church or any discussion of spiritual things, salvation, or the Bible came up, he made himself scarce. When pressed, he'd say: "You know I'm not interested in all of that."

Marge asked us to pray for Bill. At one point, God put on my heart to make intercession in prayer for Bill, especially for the "godly sorrow that works repentance."

It's never easy to witness to a spouse or close family member. Add to that the fact that Marge's religious schooling, training, and background had given her little or no clue as to a personal relationship with Christ, until she met Him for herself. Then there was certainly no background for witnessing or winning others to Christ. But with Bill at 81 years of age and diagnosed with a terminal illness, the Lord supplied Marge with the needed wisdom and words at the most needed time.

The first time I saw Bill after his salvation experience was at Alive Hospice in Nashville. He called me Brother Ed and was *right at home* when we offered prayer. He even gladly held my hand while we prayed.

The steps leading to the smiles and remarkable change in Bill's life demonstrates God's love, faithfulness and mercy.

His message is very clear: Never give up!

The sanctity of a dedicated, praying wife blesses and benefits both she and her mate for time and all eternity!

C. Ed Irwin, Assistant Pastor
Smyrna River of Life Assembly of God

INTRODUCTION

I DON'T KNOW about you, but I am a rather slow learner. I finally understood that, first, I need to wait on God. Next, I learned that when God is ready to make His move, I had better proceed and not argue.

God got me up at 1 AM to write this message of hope for you. He is the One Who wrote it. Just as He, by His Holy Spirit, directed men to write the Bible, He gave me what He wanted said in this book.

I don't refer to this as a story. Stories can be true or false, fiction or non-fiction. This was absolutely a true experience, an experience of God's grace -- and of His mercy.

This book is not about my husband and me. It is a message of hope, using our experience.

God wants you to know that He knows everything about you, and that He knows everything about the people in your life.

He knows what's in your heart and mind, and He knows what is in their heart and mind. He knows the depths of your pain - heartfelt and physical - and He knows theirs.

So as you read this, know that I love my husband. You already know that the person(s) we love the most can also be the one who pierce our heart the deepest.

As you read, you may live out some of your own experiences of past or current pains, disappointments, or frustrations. You may even feel anger and bitterness rise up in you. Just keep reading. Hang on for a short ride and come out in the Light of Hope. You'll see. God wants to tell you something.

In the meantime, I say, "Thank You, Jesus!!"

And later, you will too.

1

THE EXPERIENCE

WOW. MARRIED OVER thirty years and the name of Jesus would never cross his lips. Nope, he did not want to see any preachers and didn't even want me going to church. "What do you need that for? You don't need that!"

Yep, I was raised Catholic. For me, can't say I was saved, but I really didn't know what being saved meant anyway. Now I am not saying that Catholics aren't saved; for myself, I'm just saying that I did not know what that meant.

I remember one time back in the late 1980s or early 1990s, as I was driving home from work, I asked God, "Why didn't you give me a Christian husband?" I don't recall ever getting an answer. Later, I think it was because I wasn't really a Christian yet either. More on that later.

Another time, years later, again while driving to work, I asked, "Lord, why don't you just do Bill like you did Saul?"

Well, I did get an answer this time and it was one word: Expectation. I had to chuckle.

You see, He showed me that I was expecting the wrong thing - I wanted the Lord to do it my way (like, "Lord, do it now!"). I knew He could so why didn't He? More on that later too.

Oh, by the way, my husband's name is Bill...

WHY DID I GET an answer that time? Well, I was saved by then. Around 2006, I went with a couple of friends to a church gathering that was held in a gym.

Now, being raised Catholic where you didn't dare talk in church, I was apprehensive about what I was seeing, the way people praised God and Jesus and all.

When the time came where they asked about folks coming up and accepting Jesus as their personal Lord and Savior, I immediately sat down and said in my mind, "Lord, I ain't clean enough yet."

I cannot say that I had ever experienced the Holy Spirit before, but I can tell you that I immediately left that chair and went up front, admitted I was a sinner and asked Jesus to come live in me and be my Lord and Savior.

Wow!! Actually, at first, I didn't think anything had happened, but it had.

For example, when I had an opportunity to buy lottery scratch offs, I didn't want to play anymore. I didn't realize at the time, but that was one of the changes that happened when I asked Jesus to come live in me. He changed my heart to not want to gamble anymore.

Over time, I noticed more changes within me that I was surely glad to have. I also noticed more pin-pricks in my heart (conviction) when I thought or did something that wasn't the same thing that Jesus would think or do. After all, I was learning about what it meant to be a Christian. But I didn't realize that's what was happening.

I just knew I was changing - for the better...

I BOUGHT A KING JAMES Version Bible at some point but don't really remember when. Yep, I read that book from front to back.

Did I know what I read? Nope. I read it as a book, not as the Word of God. I had heard that the Bible was referred to as the Word of God but I still didn't really know what that meant, not until a few years later.

A guy at work loaned me a book about the Holy Spirit. It taught me that the Holy Spirit told men what to write in the Bible, and since He told them what to write, then He would guide me in what it said and meant as I read it (2 Timothy 3:16, 1 Corinthians 2:13).

That made more sense. It helped me understand what it meant as being the living Word of God, that it is really God communicating to us even today.

Over time.....

I CONTINUED TO LEARN and grow in what it meant to be a Christian and live as a Christian. I certainly wasn't and still am not perfect, but I began living as a believer, however, I was still weak in faith.

(That just means that I still believed the devil more than I believed in God's love and power, and His personally caring for me.)

I used to be embarrassed to read the Bible in front of my husband so I would wait until he went to bed or I would get up very early in the morning. I would read books by Max Lucado, Madam Guyon, Beth Moore and others. I was hungry and thirsty for the Lord but didn't know that is what it was.

Now, about that unbelieving husband...

BILL HAD A GREAT SMILE and a cute giggle. He loved to bowl and would keep people laughing. He came up with funny nicknames that stuck. He and our Boston Terrier loved to take naps together. The Boston would even come get him, reminding him that it was 2:20 PM, time for their nap.

Bill made the best cornbread I ever ate. It was always moist and flavorful. He had a secret ingredient. He also made really good chili. He had a secret ingredient for that too.

He could pick out the best birthday and anniversary cards. He would surprise people with his fabulous ability to remember their birthday and anniversary dates. I always got a Mother's Day card from the four-legged kid (whatever dog we had at the time).

Well, as I mentioned before....

WE HAD BEEN MARRIED for over thirty years. We all know what it's like living with someone: parents, siblings, spouses, children, room mates, and so on.

First, we don't really know someone until we live with them.

Second, the way they are at home isn't always the same person that folks see outside of home. Yep, what folks see is not always reality.

It's hard being married to an unbeliever, regardless. What is in folks' hearts is what they believe and what they believe is the way they act.

Anyway, over the years, my unbelieving husband was rude to me and to my family. He chose "his" family over me every time. He spoke meanly to me and was controlling. I couldn't be me, whoever that was.

Sometimes, I just wanted to die. He didn't love me. Selfish. Hurtful. Mean. Sometimes, I just cried so deeply. But, not in front of him.

Oh no, I wasn't allowed to cry in front of him...

ALL THESE YEARS, I had been trying to do everything I could to get Bill to love me (not reject me with just a look or sharp word).

The pain he delivered was all to the heart.

After all, that's what we all want: to be loved, to be accepted...

FINALLY, DURING A multi-week camping trip for our thirtieth anniversary, the Lord showed me that I had been putting Bill, my unbelieving husband, as my god instead of putting God as my God. That was a hard trip.

He showed me too that the meanness, selfishness and rudeness I saw in Bill were not the person that God created.

God created us in His image (Genesis 1:26-27) and He isn't mean or rude or selfish (Galatians 5:22, 1 John 4:8). I didn't realize it, but that was the devil's ways I was experiencing all those years.

Because Bill was an unbeliever, the devil had a good 'ole time tormenting both of us, *from different perspectives.*

Yet, I still felt stuck, very stuck, like nothing would ever change.

I would cry that deep, hurting, soulful cry...

I HAD BEEN READING the Bible and growing in faith and understanding. I had started going to church, not regularly, but going and growing.

The Lord had changed Bill enough to finally give me a break and not complain about my going to church. He would actually ask me how I liked it. I did tell him that I liked this church, that it was like the original Christian church where they don't put all their money in a building but put it where the needs of the people are, missions, etc.

He never commented, but that was okay...

SINCE I HAD BEEN GROWING in faith - believing that God means what He says in the Bible - I started praying a bit differently (Deuterotomy 7:9).

For example, the Bible says that we can come to God in the Name of Jesus and ask what we want and He would do it, so long as it is within His desire (Mark 11:24, Matthew 21:22). So, I asked God to give Bill to Jesus because Jesus said that He never loses whoever the Father gives Him (John 6:37, John 10:29).

Well, I would keep asking, "God, would You please give Bill to Jesus because He ain't gonna lose whoever You give Him."

Eventually, the Lord showed me that it was time for me to quit doubting. I was showing I was doubting because I kept asking. It was time for me to have faith and to do that, I needed to change my prayer to one of thankfulness. God loves for us to be thankful!

So, I changed my prayer to "God, thank You for giving Bill to Jesus! He belongs to You now!"

Now keep in mind, Bill didn't just jump up and suddenly believe in Jesus like Saul did. Remember, I had already asked God to do Bill like He did Saul.

Now, whenever Bill would say mean things or whatever, I would tell myself "Nope, he belongs to God now!" and that helped me to not take whatever Bill said or did personally.

But God still did not manifest His Will in Bill yet...

PART OF HAVING FAITH in God is letting go of whatever is bothering us.

So, I finally had to tell God, "Okay God. I know he is Yours because I have asked You to give him to Jesus, and I know You have because I have asked and asked in faith. I know I asked for something in Your will because You don't want any of us lost and so I know that Bill will not be lost. Now, I just have to tell Ya that whenever You do it and whoever You use to do it and wherever You do it, I just ask that You please confirm to me that it is done, that he is saved, and not let me wonder after he dies."

Yep, I had to let go of any of my own ideas on how God would accomplish Bill coming to know Jesus and believing.

I had to let go and trust that God would do His plan in His timing.

I needed to totally trust God...

EVENTUALLY, I QUIT WORK due to Bill's health. We had talked about doing a camping trip out West for years and decided to do it for our thirtieth wedding anniversary. That was the trip I mentioned earlier.

The next year, we found out about some other health issues Bill had that were terminal. Within twenty months, Bill was signed up with hospice, which usually meant maybe six months to live.

We had already taken care of funeral arrangements a few years earlier so at least we didn't have to discuss all that. We visited with family and friends early on because hospice folks told us that he would reach a point that he would not want visitors.

That was true...

BILL AND I HAD a variety of discussions, but still not about salvation.

I did ask him once about where he thought he would go when he died. He muttered something.

I told him that there really is a hell and it is much worse than war.

You see, he was in the Korean War, so he knew about being in the middle of that kind of horror.

Anyway, nothing more was said on that topic, until...

THE FRIDAY BEFORE Mother's Day, we got up late. I was getting ready to have a drink of water and the Lord put on me to do a three day fast - no food or water.

Saturday, we went for a car ride and while we were out, he got nauseous. As soon as we got home, he threw up. He was tired and lay down. He said he didn't want any company.

The next day, he wasn't feeling very well and still did not want any company. He said he was sorry he had not gotten me a card or anything for Mother's Day, from those four-legged kids I mentioned earlier.

I told him that was okay since he never really had a chance to get out and get anything, and not to worry about it. He asked about going out to eat. I told him let's wait until Monday, the next day, when it wouldn't be so crowded. He was okay with that.

That night, he asked me, "How long are we going to stay here?" We liked to travel, and I thought he was having some confusion, so I replied, "Maybe a couple more nights."

He seemed bothered but gave no other clues...

MONDAY, BILL STILL wasn't feeling very well. We started to go out but he was weak and his oxygen level was too low. The hospice nurse came by at that time and noticed that he seemed to be a bit worse than when she had seen him the week before. So he rested for a while.

He was restless and wasn't sleeping hardly at all, days or nights.

He wanted me with him all the time, and I mean ALL the time, which was unusual for him. I did need to let the dogs in and out to potty but he didn't want me gone from him for even that.

Again, it was unusual behavior for him...

TUESDAY NIGHT, around 11:30 PM, I heard him get up. He had his pants on, his shirt on backwards, was putting on his shoes and saying, "We gotta get out of here. I have to get my car keys."

I called hospice right away. He was not sleeping and was restless.

The hospice nurse came out around 2 AM. God blessed us. It was not the regular on-call nurse. It was someone who had seen Bill during the day and knew what was normal for him.

She called first to see what was going on, then called the doctor. She called back regarding some medication to give him and see if that would work before she got to the house. She had about a forty-minute drive.

The meds had not started to work quite yet when she arrived and she checked him over.

Eventually, he did fall asleep...

WE GOT UP EARLY afternoon on Wednesday. I'm sitting in a chair across from him as he is sitting on the bed.

In an unusual way and very calmly, he says, "I can't believe that after all these years that I can't trust you."

Quite surprised, I asked, "What are you talking about?"

He repeated, "I can't believe that after all these years that I can't trust you."

I asked him, "Where are you?"

He said, "In a building."

I asked, "Is it dark in there?"

He replied, "Yes."

I told him, "Baby, that's the devil and he is telling you lies about me. He's the enemy."

I sat beside him on the bed and said, "Now baby, you're going to have to say (with strong expression)

'Jesus! Come get me out of here!!'" (and repeated that) and told him that he would need to say that out loud.

He muttered something. Then he said lazily, "Jesus, can You get me out of here?"

I said, "No baby, you gotta say, Jesus, come get me out of here!"

He muttered something again, and in the meantime we moved from the bedroom to the living room.

As we did, I sent a text to some prayer warriors, "The devil is after Bill! Got spiritual warfare going on! Need prayers now!"

Bill sat in his rocker, and I sat in a chair across from him. I knew the spiritual skirmish was a full-on war.

While sitting there, I said, "Bill, you remember when you were in the Korean War and you were in reconnaissance behind enemy lines and you didn't know if they were going to fire on you or what and how afraid you were?"

He replied, "Yeah, and that's the kind of fear I'm having now." (that's some really bad fear, and it confirmed that he was being embraced by evil).

I said, "Okay, baby, you know how also that you could call in the artillery and they would fire on the enemy?"

He replied, "Yes."

I said, "Well, okay baby, I've called in the artillery. I have prayer warriors right now praying and firing on the enemy."

My brother called (he's a pastor) and gave me a couple of scriptures to read to him. I read those aloud.

> *John 3:16 "For God so loved the world, that he gave his only begotten Son, that whosoever believeth in him should not perish, but have everlasting life."*
>
> *John 14:6 "Jesus saith unto him, I am the way, the truth and the life; no man cometh unto the Father but by me."*

I also told him, "The unbelieving husband is sanctified by the believing wife." (1 Corinthians 7:14) I didn't recall the book, chapter and verse, but the Lord brought that scripture to mind to tell him.

At that point, the skirmish was over but I knew the battle wasn't done...

EARLY THURSDAY MORNING, he sat on the side of the bed, me in the chair across from him, and he said in that calm but unusual voice, "You know I'm disappointed."

I asked him, "Are you in that dark place again?"

He said, "Yes. Why did you bring me here?"

I said, "Baby, I didn't bring you there."

He replied, "You mean I'm here by myself?"

I said, "Yes baby. You're there alone and I can't help you. There is only one way out and I can't help you. You're going to have to say (emphatic voice here) "Jesus! Come help me! Jesus! Come help me!" You're going to have to say that out loud, several times."

So, we both said it out loud. I'm sitting across from him, my hands on his legs, but my head is down and my eyes are closed.

After we both said that out loud several times, I said, "Okay baby, now you're going to have to say out loud (emphatically here again), "I believe You Jesus!! I believe You Jesus!!" and say it out loud, and say it several times."

So, we both did.

Next I said, "Okay baby, now we say, "Thank You Jesus!! Thank You Jesus!!", and we did, several times, out loud.

Jesus literally had rescued Bill, my *previously unbelieving husband,* from the clutches of satan.

Hang on! There's more to this beautiful experience!!

THE HOSPICE NURSE came late that morning. She sat on the bed with Bill sitting beside her. I told her what happened that morning and she's crying and I'm crying and we are so excited!

Once we finished and settled down, she discussed the situation and asked if we had considered that it is probably time for Bill to go to the Hospice Residence. We both agreed so she began the approval process.

In the meantime, Bill's doctor and nurse came for a personal visit. They sat on the bed across from Bill.

Bill said, "Tell them what happened this morning!'

So, I told them. At the end of my telling the experience (it's not a story so I'm not calling it a story), I said to Bill, "And you aint in that dark place anymore are ya baby?"

And he replied, "No, and I saw Light!"

Later, the hospice nurse commented about the glow that Bill had...

SHE FINALIZED arrangements and the ambulance came to get him.

The nurse updated the Residence nurse on all of Bill's details. Shortly, the Residence nurse called back and said she forgot to ask one question, what is Bill's religious preference?

Our hospice nurse smiled and replied that he is Christian, a new Christian as of today!

AT SOME POINT, I sent texts to our prayer warriors to let them know about Bill's salvation.

I packed up some things to take to the Hospice Residence. Once there, I met our granddaughter (an awesome Christian young woman). While we are at the bathroom sink with Bill, the Lord impressed upon her to baptize him right then.

So she did!

As soon as he got baptized, he said, "Praise the Lord!"

Man, are we ecstatic! To get to hear this from someone who never believed!

We got him back into the wheelchair and handed him some oxygen tubing (it kept him busy during his restlessness). He sat up and started talking about we need to love the children and families, etc.

He was prophesying! He was speaking whatever the Lord was telling him directly.

He mentioned this nation, the United States, local governments, not many days. He ended with "Welcome aboard."

The Lord welcomed him aboard!

THAT NIGHT WAS VERY ROUGH. I had gone home to get some clothes and come back. I initially wasn't planning on staying the night because he was in good hands, and I needed rest and time with the dogs.

Well, Bill was in both the physical and spiritual worlds. He saw spiritual things, would reach out to them, move his eyes and head to follow them, even saluted once.

They didn't think he was going to make it through the night. I didn't either. Finally around 3 AM, they gave him some really strong medicine and knocked him out.

Friday afternoon, the doctor said he may have twelve, twenty-four or maybe thirty-six hours to live. She said she would be surprised if he were still here on Monday.

I cried. I notified folks. I called about the casket. I called the funeral home...

Surprisingly on Saturday, he was alert and eating. He made a comment at one point that he "hopes He will forgive me of things I've done in the past."

I made a note of that and discussed it with a beautiful Christian friend. She guided me on specific scriptures of confess, ask forgiveness and repent (1 John 1:9).

I kept that in mind...

MY ASSOCIATE PASTOR, Brother Ed, was always asking about Bill and about coming by the house during the several years before. He prayed a lot for Bill's salvation.

Bill saw him once several years earlier but never really wanted to see him again, until...

WHEN BROTHER ED CAME to the Hospice Residence, I told him what happened that Thursday morning. Bless his heart. He had big 'ole tears in his eyes as he heard about the experience.

After the nurse finished giving Bill his bath, Brother Ed and I went into the room, standing on each side of the bed. Bill smiled and was glad to see him. Brother Ed spoke for a few minutes, then asked Bill if he could pray with him. Bill lifted his hand to Brother Ed's and we prayed!

That was such a wonderful experience.

SUNDAY, HE WAS AWAKE SOME but not as good as the day before. Monday and Tuesday, he was out, completely asleep and could not be awakened.

Again, the doctor didn't expect him to be alive by Wednesday.

He was. Everyone was surprised.

At one point, he told us that he had joined the Church of Jesus Christ and Soldiers. I was shocked to even hear him say he joined a church.

I was also elated...

REMEMBER I MENTIONED THAT he was concerned if he would be forgiven of his past?

Later that evening I asked Bill if he recalled making the comment. He did.

So I told him, "Well Bill, there are three things we need to do. You know how dirty you feel about the stuff you did in the past? I feel the same way for mine too. Well, we need to do these three things out loud, okay?"

He said okay.

"First, we need to confess our sins out loud. We don't have to be specific, but we can be general. So we will go 'God, You know all I did in the past and I confess it to You now and I know I did wrong.'" So he did this out loud.

"Next, we ask out loud for forgiveness." So he did.

Last, I told him, "Now we repent which means we won't do those things again."

As soon as he did that out loud, he raised his hands, rubbed them together and wiped them clean! I could tell he was white as snow at that point! And he knew he was too...

SOMETIMES, WHEN BILL WAS awake and when one of the Residence staff came in, I would get the sense that the Lord would have something to tell them.

So I would ask Bill, "Do you have a message for" this person (whoever it was there). Then he would close his eyes, focus on the Lord, and give a personal message from the Lord to that person.

It was so precious and beautiful to see Bill pray, how he would close his eyes, focus on Jesus, and say His Name and pray his prayer.

Also of significance, was to truly see the new man. His face was child-like and sweet and with a glow he never had before.

God has blessed us so much at this point, but we aren't through yet...

BY THURSDAY, BILL IS wanting to go home. And I mean, he *REALLY* wants to go home.

The hospice folks and I had some concern about his coming home because he had been in bed and not walked in a week, and didn't expect him to even be around (twice) by this point.

So we agreed to let him sit on the side of the bed and eventually in a chair. It was priceless to watch him pat the floor with his feet, like a little child.

He sat in the chair for a while...

BY DINNER TIME, I'm starting to get a bit anxious about his wanting to go home.

I finally lose it and said, "Bill!! We thought you were going to die here at hospice and now you want to go home! That's a 180-degree turn and I have a lot to see about and see if we can handle it at home! Bill, I just need for you to pray for me!"

And he did, beautifully! Now as always, he closed his eyes, focused on Jesus, and said "Jesus," and then his prayer.

Once he finished praying, he said, "I hope I did that right."

I said, "Baby, ya did good. That was just right. Ya know, God needed me to see that He handles the details as well as the big things and all things in between. Thank you baby."

Then he told me not to be upset, that, "You're the only one I have."

I told him, "You've got Jesus now baby!"

But he replied, "You're the only human I have." I never asked what he meant.

WELL, HE REALLY WANTS to go home. This is the Friday before Memorial weekend.

The doctor and nurse practitioner were thinking about waiting until after Monday, Memorial Day.

So I went home, thinking I would get some clothes and return. However, I saw we already had all we needed, and I prayed about it. When I got back to Bill, I told him we would see if we could convince the doctor that we were good for him to go home.

Once the doctor and nurse practitioner came in, we convinced them we were okay for Bill to go home. They needed to see if they could get the additional equipment he needed to be home with. If that could be done, then we could go that evening.

After they left the room, what did Bill do?

He prayed. "Jesus, please make it happen for me to get to go home. Thank You Jesus. Amen."

The nurse came back and said they could get what they needed by 7 PM, and that I would need to go home and be there for some medicine that needed to be delivered.

Once she left the room, we were glad that it was going to work out.

So, what did Bill do?

He prayed. "Thank You Jesus for making it happen for me to get to go home. Amen."

He didn't want me to have to leave. He wanted me with him all the time, in a loving way now. But he understood that I needed to go home to sign for the medicine being delivered.

So, I went home, anxiously awaiting...

BILL MADE IT HOME around 9 PM. He went downhill quickly after that but at least he was home.

One of the dogs that liked to nap with him got to sleep with him a couple of nights.

Saturday, we went around the house, him in a wheelchair. I gave him a haircut and a bath.

He was very glad to be home. I was very glad too...

BY SUNDAY, HE PRAYED, "Jesus, please help me out of this situation. Jesus, please help me out of this situation. Thank You Jesus."

Later that day, out of the clear, Bill said, "I don't know how to ride a horse but I can learn."

I made a mental note of his comment. I knew he saw someone I couldn't see...

BILL JOINED JESUS' ARMY of soldiers around 7:53 AM that Thursday morning. He went to learn how to ride that horse in the Lord's army.

Several times before he died, I would pat his hand and tell him that his experience would give many others hope, many would be saved, and that we would get his experience out to people all over the world.

God gave me a Christian husband after all.

And I say, "Thank You Jesus!"

2

THE MESSAGE

THERE ARE SEVERAL THINGS the Lord wants you to know from our experience.

This message is for EVERYONE, not just for believing wives. It is for parents for your children. It is for believing husbands for your wife. It is for children for your parents. It is for believing coworkers for your unbelieving coworkers. It is for Christians to renew their faith and hope and refocus on what it means to truly follow Jesus.

† Hope

Never ever give up hope. God always answers prayers. He just may have a different plan than the one we have in mind for the answer.

(Romans 15:13, Jeremiah 29:11)

† Thanksgiving

Once you ask in faith, believe it is done and change your prayer to one of thanksgiving. Believe and let go. Do not fret or worry anymore. Change your worry to thanksgiving.

(Philippians 4:6, Psalms 136:1)

† Forgiveness

Part of the experience with Bill not mentioned above is about forgiveness. With several of us in the room, I talked about the fact that there is anger and bitterness, and the only way to be totally free of that burden is to forgive. I told them that I had had a lot of anger and bitterness toward my mom, but one day, I called her and forgave her. I told them about the freedom that I had gotten from that. Bill and I forgave each other right there and then.

(Matthew 6:14-15, Mark 11:25, Luke 6:37)

† Believe

We can't receive what God wants to give us until we really believe - believe that He really does love you. Believe that He really does want to bless you. Once you believe, then you can receive all God has to give you.

(Jeremiah 29:12-13, Matthew 12:22, Hebrews 11:6, John 1:12, Psalm 40:5, Romans 6:23)

† Trust

God wants you to know that you can trust Him in *all* areas of your living. He knows the big things, the details, and all the stuff in between - always - not just occasionally. He knows it for everyone, everywhere, all the time.

(Hebrews 4:13, Psalm 139:1-7, Psalm 37:5)

3

WHO ARE WE?

I GUESS YOU MAY BE wondering about 'the rest of the story' as Paul Harvey used to say. Actually, it is more like 'who are we', my husband Bill and I.

BUT FIRST...

In some ways, everyone wants and needs exactly the same thing. We all want to be loved. We all want to be accepted. We all want to have that sense of fulfillment.

So, I guess we are all alike, at least in those things.

After all, God created us all in His image (Genesis 1:27). Therefore, we are all alike - to a point.

How we try to find those things reminds me of a song back in the '80s, "Lookin' for Love in All the Wrong Places," sung by Johnny Lee.

Yep, I kept looking for that love and acceptance from Bill, for a whole lot of years (remember, over thirty-two years). I thought that if I received that, then I would have that sense of fulfillment, too. What else is needed?

Yep, I was lookin' for love in all the wrong places.

THE PART I HAVEN'T TOLD you yet is that there was over twenty-six years age difference between Bill and me. Yep, he was just over four months older than my mother, and about a year and a half younger than my dad.

We actually had a Protestant preacher turn us down to marry us. He said something about 'these young women looking for father figures.' I wasn't looking to marry my dad!

Oh, I also hadn't mentioned how long we dated before we got married - only four months. Yep, you never know what God may have planned for you, that's for sure.

No, it wasn't a 'shotgun' wedding, a saying in the South. I was not pregnant and we did not HAVE to get married. As a matter of fact, before I met Bill, I considered becoming a nun! But, God had other plans.

I didn't mention any of this before because, well, this information just is not important to the message that God wants in this book.

As I mentioned in the Introduction, God is the One who woke me up to write 'The Experience'. The content is what the Lord had my fingers dancing on the keyboard to write.

YOU MAY ALSO BE WONDERING how and when I knew what to say to Bill that morning during his salvation experience.

I didn't.

I couldn't see what Bill was seeing. I couldn't experience what he was experiencing.

The Lord knew though. The Lord provided all that. I had no thoughts of my own. I was merely the pass-through vessel of the Lord's work for Bill's salvation.

YOU SEE, GOD ANSWERED my prayers in multiple ways and exceedingly so.

Remember, I had to let go and give God my concern about knowing if and when Bill would be saved. I had no idea that He would use me the way He did. Of course, I'm excited and very humbled that He did.

AS TIME HAS PASSED, God used Bill to teach me some things I needed to learn.

For example, I didn't realize that God loves all of us, no matter what, and that He truly listens – heart to heart.

Now too, I say, "Thank You Jesus!" in the same way that we did that first time. Thanking Jesus is a much deeper thing for me now.

I have learned how important it is to let go and trust God.

God taught me that He really does know everything, and that I don't have to know things. I just need to be quiet, listen and trust Him for absolutely everything.

BUT THESE ARE NOT just for me.

God did all this *for you* and *for Bill* and *for me*. He doesn't want anyone lost for eternity (2 Peter 3:9).

I learned that God personally cares for me, and for each of us, and that He is so precious and awesome. He is our fulfillment, and only He can fulfill that deep, seeking part of our heart and soul (Psalm 138:8, Psalm 57:2).

4

WHAT DOES GOD WANT US TO KNOW?

To Those Who Believe

FIRST, KNOW THAT GOD DEEPLY loves you (John 3:16).

He knows your heart's desires. In Psalm 37:4-5, it says, "Delight thyself also in the Lord: and he shall give thee the desires of thine heart. Commit thy way unto the Lord; trust also in him; and he shall bring it to pass."

It is important to our Father that you give Him all of your cares and *leave them* with Him. God our Father already knows all things and His timing is always perfect (1 Peter 5:7).

From His heart, He desires your trust in Him. You know that our Father does not want anyone lost to hell, but it is up to each *individual*. He tells us that truth in John 3:15-16: "That *whosoever* believeth in him should not perish, but have eternal life. For God so loved the world, that he gave his only begotten Son, that *whosoever* believeth in him should not perish, but have everlasting life." (italics mine)

When you pray and ask the Father, ask Him in faith with sincerity from the depths of your heart. Then just keep believing Him and thanking Him (Matthew 21:22).

Our Father loves you so much that He sent Jesus to receive His wrath to pay for your sins and for all sin. Can you imagine how hard it was for Him to have to take away His Presence from Jesus, to forsake Him (Matthew 27:46)?

But Jesus loves you so much, too, that He willingly died so you and the Father and all of heaven could be together forever.

To Those Who Do Not Believe

So, where do you think you will go when your earthly body dies (Mark 16:16)?

God created every person in His image and breathed life into you so you do have a spirit.

There is only one of two places you can go:

To be with the Father forever in **heaven**

(John 14:1-3),

or

To be tormented forever in **hell** where your senses will be keener, where you will feel pain forever, where you will thirst forever, where you will wish you could truly be dead but you won't ever die.

God does not want anyone to go there.

But, *you* are the only one who can *choose* which place you will go (Romans 10:13).

To Everyone

God loves of each us regardless of what any of us has done.

There is one way to heaven, *only one* (John 14:6).

"For God so loved the world, that he gave his only begotten Son, that whosoever believeth in him should not perish, but have everlasting life." (John 3:16).

Jesus is the example for how to have a relationship with our Father in heaven. Thank You Jesus for showing each of us how to love one another and how to live!

5

WHAT DOES IT MEAN TO "BE SAVED?"

I NEVER REALLY KNEW before what was meant by 'to be saved.' I do now, especially since I saw it so clearly with Bill's salvation experience.

So, God wanted to add this chapter to help the unbeliever get the picture.

Saved FROM What?

Have you read the book *23 Minutes in Hell: One Man's Story About What He Saw, Heard, and Felt in that Place of Torment* by Bill Weise?

It is a true description and experience of hell. It is not just a place; *it is an eternal experience*. It is a fulltime experience of pain, hate, torment and thirst (Matthew 25:41, Matthew 13:49-50, 2 Peter 2:4, Mark 9:43).

God's Presence is not there, so none of His personal characteristics are there either - no love, no peace, no joy, no comfort (2 Thessalonians 1:6-9).

Anyone who is not certain about what happens after life here, or even anyone that is certain, could benefit from reading that book.

Hell is worse than anything we could ever, ever experience here. It is total separation from God forever.

By the way, it lasts *forever*. I keep repeating the word 'forever' because the realization of that truth is so very important.

Did the 1 Corinthians 7:14 verse, about the unbelieving husband is sanctified by the believing wife, provide salvation for Bill because of my believing?

Absolutely not!

Salvation is an individual event by individual choice. My husband had to call on Jesus and believe in Him and Who He is (Rom 10:13).

I couldn't do that for him.

Saved FOR What?

Jesus said He went to prepare a place for us (John 14:1-3). To exist in heaven will be greater than anything we could ever imagine.

To live forever, having incorruptible treasures (Matthew 6:20).

No more tears, no more pain, no more sorrow - ever again (Revelation 21:4).

What Do I Need To Do To Be Saved?

No one comes to the Father but by Me (John 14:6). Believe that Jesus is the Son of God, that He came in the flesh, and that He died on the cross and rose from the dead. He took upon Himself all of our sins. Say out loud:

> Jesus, I admit that I am a sinner. You know that I have tried to fix myself on my own, over and over.
>
> Jesus, I just can't do it. I'm tired and am ready for a forever change.
>
> Jesus, You're the only One Who can do this, the only One Who can set my heart and my soul straight. You're the only One Who has already paid for these sins of mine.
>
> Jesus, will You please come now?
>
> Jesus, will You please come live in my heart, and be my Lord and Savior?

With all my heart, I ask.

With all my heart, I believe You Jesus.

Thank You Jesus! Amen!

Your salvation includes *total and forever* forgiveness of your sins, as well as your total healing.

Love God, not worldly things. Jesus commands us to love one another (John 13:34-35).

Trust God. He loves you SO much!

Start by reading and studying the Bible and getting to know Him. Join up with other Christians who live and walk in the ways of Jesus, not the ways of the world.

It's not religion that God wants. It's an intimate, honest and deep relationship He wants – with you and with every person.

Praise God constantly. He will bless you!

You will be amazed at the changes in your heart, the way you think and act. You will have a kind of freedom you've never had before.

And you too will say, 'Thank You Jesus!"

Will you still occasionally do wrong? Certainly! We all do! We live in an imperfect world.

But that's when we go back to God. He is waiting for us to return to Him with a repentant heart. It's ok. He never, ever leaves us.

He is faithful to us - always.

SCRIPTURE REFERENCES

THESE ARE THE SCRIPTURES that are referenced in the book. These were put at the end so they would not distract your flow as you read.

Mainly for those not familiar with the order of the books in the Bible, I put these in alphabetical sequence so they would be easier to find.

1 Corinthians 2:13 Which things also we speak, not in the words which man's wisdom teacheth, but which the Holy Ghost teacheth; comparing spiritual things with spiritual.

1 Corinthians 7:14 For the unbelieving husband is sanctified by the wife, and the unbelieving wife is sanctified by the husband: else were your children unclean; but now are they holy.

Deuteronomy 7:9 Know therefore that the Lord thy God, he is God, the faithful God, which keepeth covenant and mercy with them that love him and keep his commandments to a thousand generations;

Galatians: 5:22-23 But the fruit of the Spirit is love, joy, peace, longsuffering, gentleness, goodness, faith, 23 Meekness, temperance...

Genesis 1:27 So God created man in his own image, in the image of God created he him; male and female created he them.

Hebrews 4:13 Neither is there any creature that is not manifest in his sight: but all things are naked and opened unto the eyes of him with whom we have to do.

Hebrews 11:6 But without faith it is impossible to please him: for he that cometh to God must believe that he is, and that he is a rewarder of them that diligently seek him.

Jeremiah 29:11 For I know the thoughts that I think toward you, saith the Lord, thoughts of peace, and not of evil, to give you an expected end.

Jeremiah 29:12-13 Then shall ye call upon me, and ye shall go and pray unto me, and I will hearken unto you. 13 And ye shall seek me, and find me, when ye shall search for me with all your heart.

John 1:12 But as many as received him, to them gave he power to become the sons of God, even to them that believe on his name:

John 3:15-16 (Jesus speaking) That whosoever believeth in him should not perish, but have eternal life. For God so loved the world, that he gave his only begotten Son, that whosoever believeth in him should not perish, but have everlasting life.

John 6:37 (Jesus speaking) All that the Father giveth me shall come to me; and him that cometh to me I will in no wise cast out.

John 10:29 (Jesus speaking) My Father, which gave them me, is greater than all; and no man is able to pluck them out of my Father's hand.

John 13:34-35 (Jesus speaking) A new commandment I give unto you, That ye love one another; as I have love you, that ye also love one another. 35 By this shall all men know that ye are my disciples, if you love one to another.

John 14:1-3 (Jesus speaking) Let not your heart be troubled: ye believe in God, believe also in me. 2 In my Father's house are many mansions: if it were not so, I would have told you. I go to prepare a place for you. 3 And if I go and prepare a place for you, I will come again, and receive you unto myself; that where I am, there ye may be also.

John 14:6 Jesus saith unto him, I am the way, the truth, and the life: no man cometh unto the Father, but by me.

1 John 4:8 He that loveth not knoweth not God; for God is love.

Luke 6:37 (Jesus speaking) Judge not, and ye shall not be judged; condemn not, and ye shall not be condemned; forgive, and ye shall be forgiven.

Mark 9:43 (Jesus speaking) And if thy hand offend thee, cut if off: it is better for thee to enter into life maimed, than having two hands to go into hell, into the fire that never shall be quenched:

Mark 11:24 (Jesus speaking) Therefore I say unto you, What things soever ye desire, when ye pray, believe that ye receive them, and ye shall have them.

Mark 11:25-26 (Jesus speaking) And when ye stand praying, forgive, if ye have ought against any; that your Father also which is in heaven may forgive you your trespasses. 26 But if ye do not forgive, neither will your Father which is in heaven forgive your trespasses.

Mark 16:16 (Jesus speaking) He that believeth and is baptized shall be saved; but he that believeth not shall be damned.

Matthew 6:14-15 (Jesus speaking) For if ye forgive men their trespasses, your heavenly Father will also forgive you; 15 But if ye forgive not men their trespasses, neither will your Father forgive your trespasses.

Matthew 6:20 (Jesus speaking) But lay up for yourselves treasure in heaven, where neither moth nor rust doth corrupt, and where thieves do not break through nor steal;

Matthew 13:49-50 (Jesus speaking) So shall it be at the end of the world: the angels shall come forth, and sever the wicked from among the just, 50 And shall cast them into the furnace of fire: there shall be wailing and gnashing of teeth.

Matthew 21:22 (Jesus speaking) And all things, whatsoever ye shall ask in prayer, believing, ye shall receive

Matthew 25:41 (Jesus speaking) Then shall he say also unto them on the left hand, Depart from me, ye cursed, into everlasting fire, prepared for the devil and his angels.

Matthew 27:46 And about the ninth hour Jesus cried with a loud voice, saying, E'li, E'li, la'ma sa-bach-tha'ni? That is to say, My God, my God, why has thou forsaken me?

1 Peter 5:7 Casting all your care upon him; for he careth for you.

2 Peter 2:4 For if God spared not the angels that sinned, but cast them down to hell, and delivered them into chains of darkness, to be reserved unto judgement;

2 Peter 3:9 The Lord is not slack concerning his promise, as some men count slackness; but is longsuffering to us-ward, not willing that any should perish, but that all should come to repentance.

Philippians 4:6 Be careful for nothing; but in every thing by prayer and supplication with thanksgiving let your requests be made known unto God.

Psalm 37:4-5 Delight thyself also in the Lord: and he shall give thee the desires of thine heart. Commit thy way unto the Lord; trust also in him; and he shall bring it to pass.

Psalm 40:5 Many, O Lord my God, are thy wonderful works which thou has done, and thy thoughts which are to us-ward; they cannot be reckoned up in order unto thee; if I would declare and speak of them, they are more than can be numbered.

Psalm 57:2 I will cry unto God most high; unto God that performeth all things for me.

Psalms 136:1 O give thanks unto the Lord; for he is good; for his mercy endureth for ever.

Psalm 138:8 The Lord will perfect that which concerneth me: thy mercy, O Lord, endureth for ever: forsake not the works of thine own hands.

Psalm 139: 1-7 O Lord, thou has searched me, and known me. 2 Thou knowest my downsitting and mine uprising, thou understandest my thought afar off. 3 Thou compassest my path and my lying down, and art acquainted with all my ways. 4 for there is not a word in my tongue, but, lo, O Lord, thou knowest it altogether. 5 Thou has beset me behind and before, and laid thine hand upon me. 6 Such knowledge is too wonderful for me; it is

high, I cannot attain unto it. 7 Whither shall I go
from thy spirit? Or whither shall I flee from thy
presence?

Revelation 21:4 And God shall wipe away all tears from their eyes; and there shall be no more death, neither sorrow, nor crying, neither shall there be any more pain: for the former things are passed away.

Romans 6:23 For the wages of sin is death; but the gift of God is eternal life through Jesus Christ our Lord.

Romans 10:13 For whosoever shall call upon the name of the Lord shall be saved.

Romans 15:13 Now the God of hope fill you with all joy and peace in believing, that ye may abound in hope, through the power of the Holy Ghost.

2 Thessalonians 1:6-9 Seeing it is a righteous
thing with God to recompense tribulation to them
that trouble you; 7 And to you who are troubled
rest with us, when the Lord Jesus shall be revealed
from heaven with his mighty angels, 8 In flaming

fire taking vengeance on them that know not God, and that obey not the gospel of our Lord Jesus Christ: 9 Who shall be punished with everlasting destruction from the presence of the Lord, and from the glory of his power;

2 Timothy 3:16 All scripture is given by inspiration of God, and is profitable for doctrine, for reproof, for correction, for instruction in righteousness:

FOR FURTHER INFORMATION

GOD DOES NOT WANT anyone to perish (2 Peter 3:9).

As a servant of God our Father and our Lord Jesus Christ, I am available to share God's love and faithfulness. Please contact me.

May God bless you abundantly!

UnbelievingHusband@gmail.com

YOUR GRACE EXPERIENCE JOURNEY NOTES

YOU MAY ALREADY HAVE had a similar experience of seeing God's grace by answering your prayer for salvation for a family member, friend, coworker or someone else. Start your notes so you can begin your book.

Begin writing notes of your own experiences - the pain, the joys, the deep soul despairing moments, the ultimately answered prayers.

I praise God that He blesses you with wisdom, knowledge, faith and joy. Ask. He will answer, in His timing, and He answers abundantly!

ABOUT THE AUTHOR

Marge is ordinary like everyone else. Yet, just like everyone else, she wants to be loved, accepted - like maybe she is valuable. Through her experience throughout childhood, and in her marriage, she had no idea. But, through answered prayer for her unbelieving husband, she began a journey she never expected. Follow along. Get set free.

MARGE and Bill GRAY were married over thirty-two years. They lived in the Nashville, Tennessee area for seventeen years. God led Marge to attend Charis Bible College in Woodland Park, Colorado.

Previously, she worked over twenty-five years in the computer industry as a programmer, project leader and in management. She worked at Federal Express and the State of Tennessee. In addition, Marge has taught several college classes.

With a servant's heart, she is a speaker, teacher, author, and editor.

CPSIA information can be obtained
at www.ICGtesting.com
Printed in the USA
BVHW031007130919
558391BV00006B/20/P